T0028323
the coop
the barn

ASSHOLES
need love too

Archimedes' Printing Shoppe
& Sundry Goodes

ASSHOLES
need love too

S.J. Russell & Erica Brown
illustrated by Maggie McMahon

ISBN 978-0-9962994-0-4
By S.J. Russell and Erica Brown
Illustrations by Maggie McMahon
Photography by Peggy Jackson
Edited by Lucy Noland

Design by A Little Graphix
Titles and text in Good Dog and Chandler 42

FIRST EDITION

Publisher's Cataloging-in-Publication Data

Names: Russell, S. J., author. | Brown, Erica Newell, author. | McMahon,
Maggie Kathleen, illustration.
Title: Assholes need love too / S. J. Russell and Erica Brown ; illustrated
by Maggie McMahon.
Description: Philadelphia, PA: Archimedes' Printing Shoppe & Sundry Goodes LLC, 2020.
Identifiers: LCCN: 2020900808 | ISBN: 978-0-9962994-0-4
Subjects: LCSH Pigs—Fiction. | Roosters—Fiction. | Dogs—Fiction. | Domestic
animals—Fiction. | Farm life—Fiction. | Animal rescue—Fiction. | BISAC FICTION /
Animals
Classification: LCC PS3618.U7675 A88 2020 | DDC 813.6--dc23

TREES.ORG FOR THE FUTURE Printed on tree-free bamboo paper stock with soy-based eco-friendly
inks in China. Cover and spine are 100% recycled Eska(R)board.

For assholes everywhere,
and those who love them.

ASSHOLES
need love too

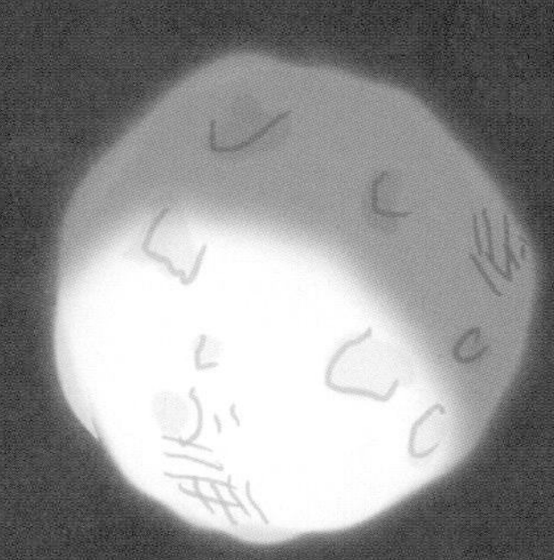

It was the dead of night.

If the blackness engulfing the New Jersey farmhouse could have been described as a color, it would have been described as. . . well . . .

BLACK.

Crickets chirped. They chirped incessantly.

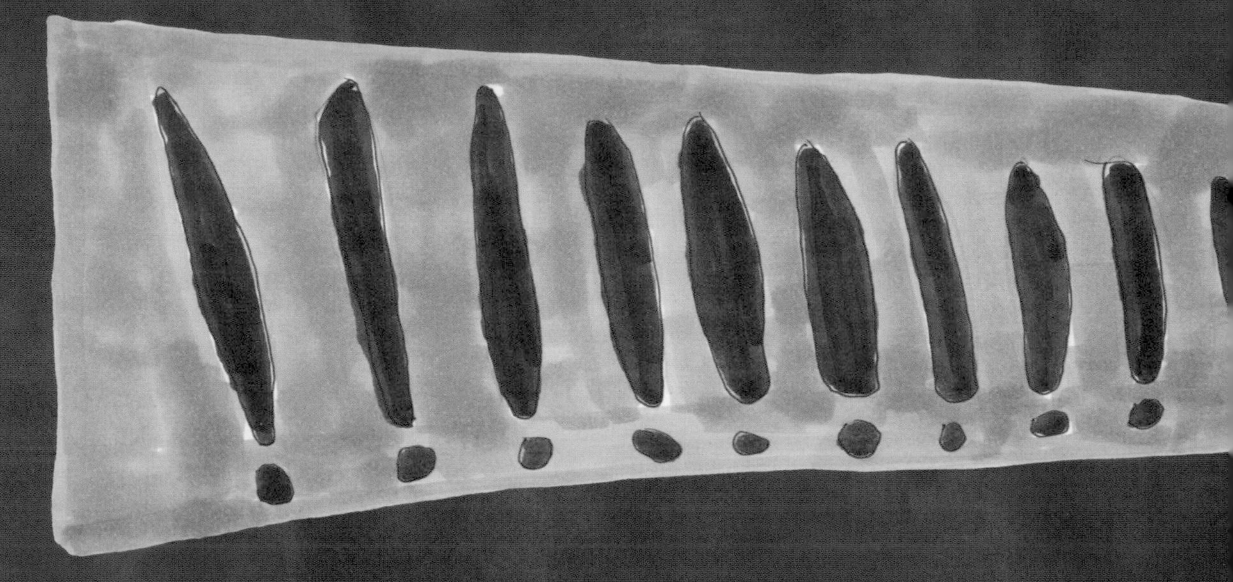

"Shut the f*ck up," yelled Wilbur to the chirping blackness.

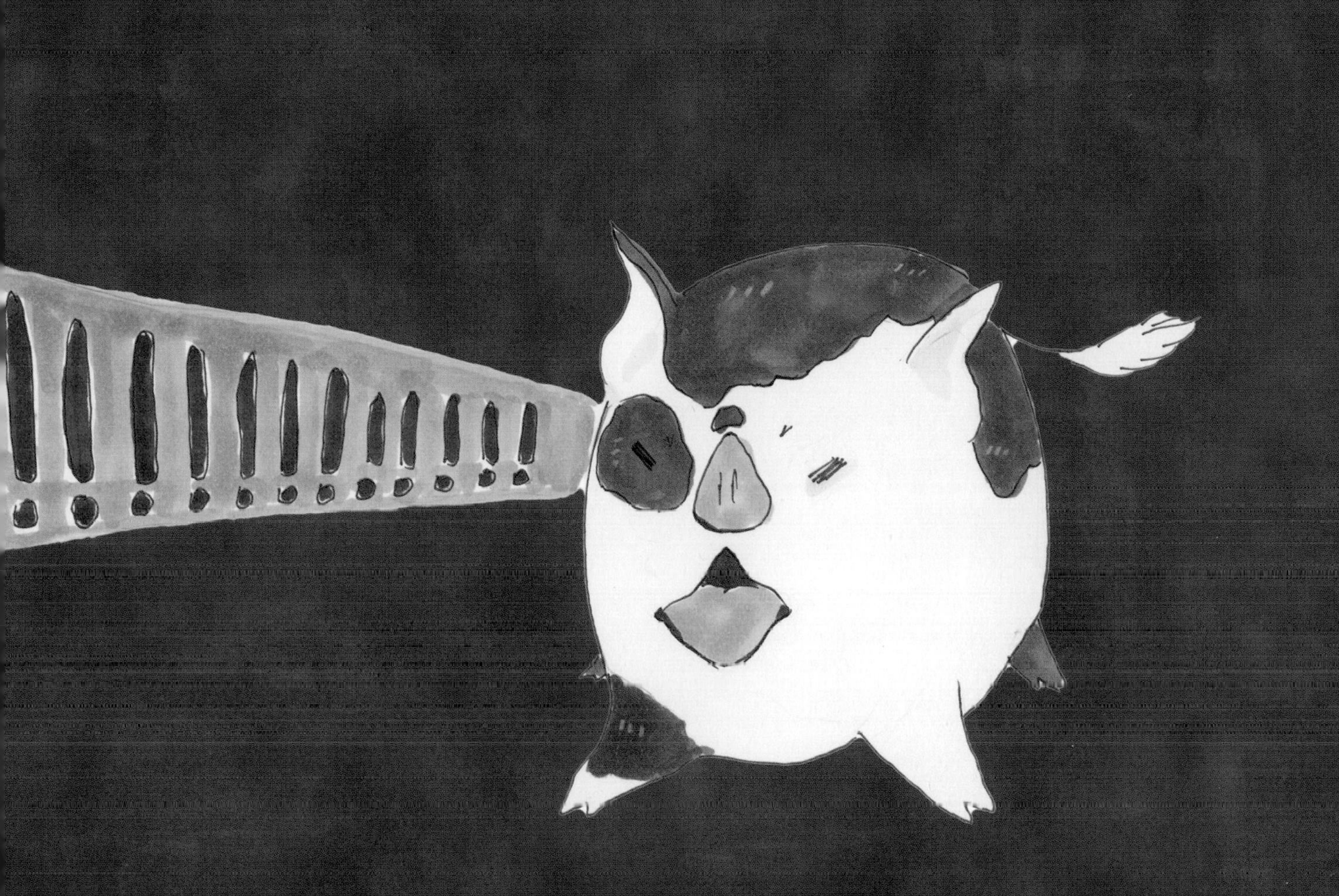

That night Wilbur had been wandering for at least an hour.

His stubby legs were tired.

He was alone for the first time.

Because he'd abandoned his children.

"This feels soooo good," said Wilbur, walking aimlessly, unable to see a thing.

Suddenly, he smelled something. Old BBQ?

It didn't matter. He wanted it.

"I'm getting me some of that," he muttered and wandered toward the smell.

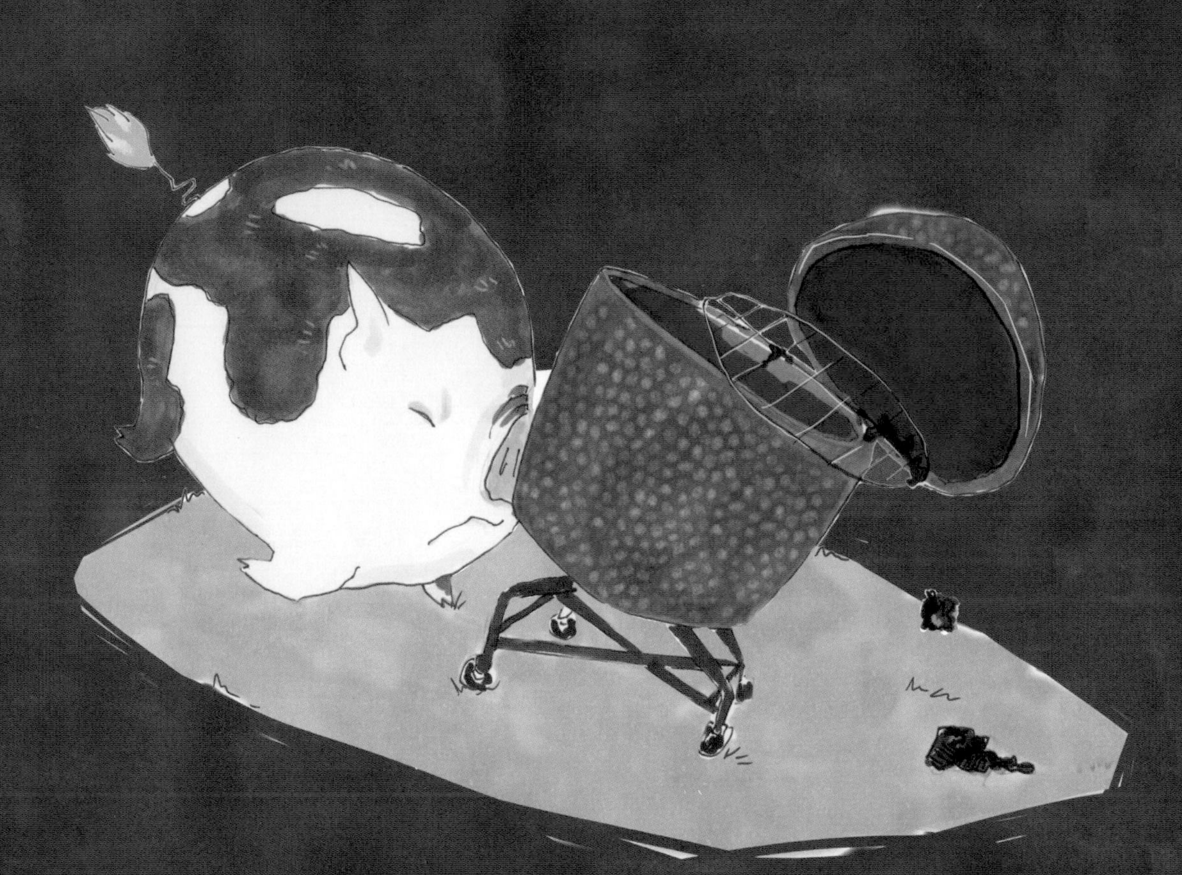

He stumbled into a big green BBQ. It toppled to the ground.

"Sh*t," cursed Wilbur.

The grill slid away. Wilbur followed the smell.

And began licking the grill.

"Ohhhh yeah," he murmured, savoring the burnt poultry and charcoal.

Suddenly lights blasted his dim vision, and a woman burst out of a door.

"Holy sh*t it's a pig!" the woman screamed to no one in particular.

"Duh," said Wilbur rolling his eyes.

When he looked up, he realized he was on the woman's back deck.

He didn't care. He kept eating.

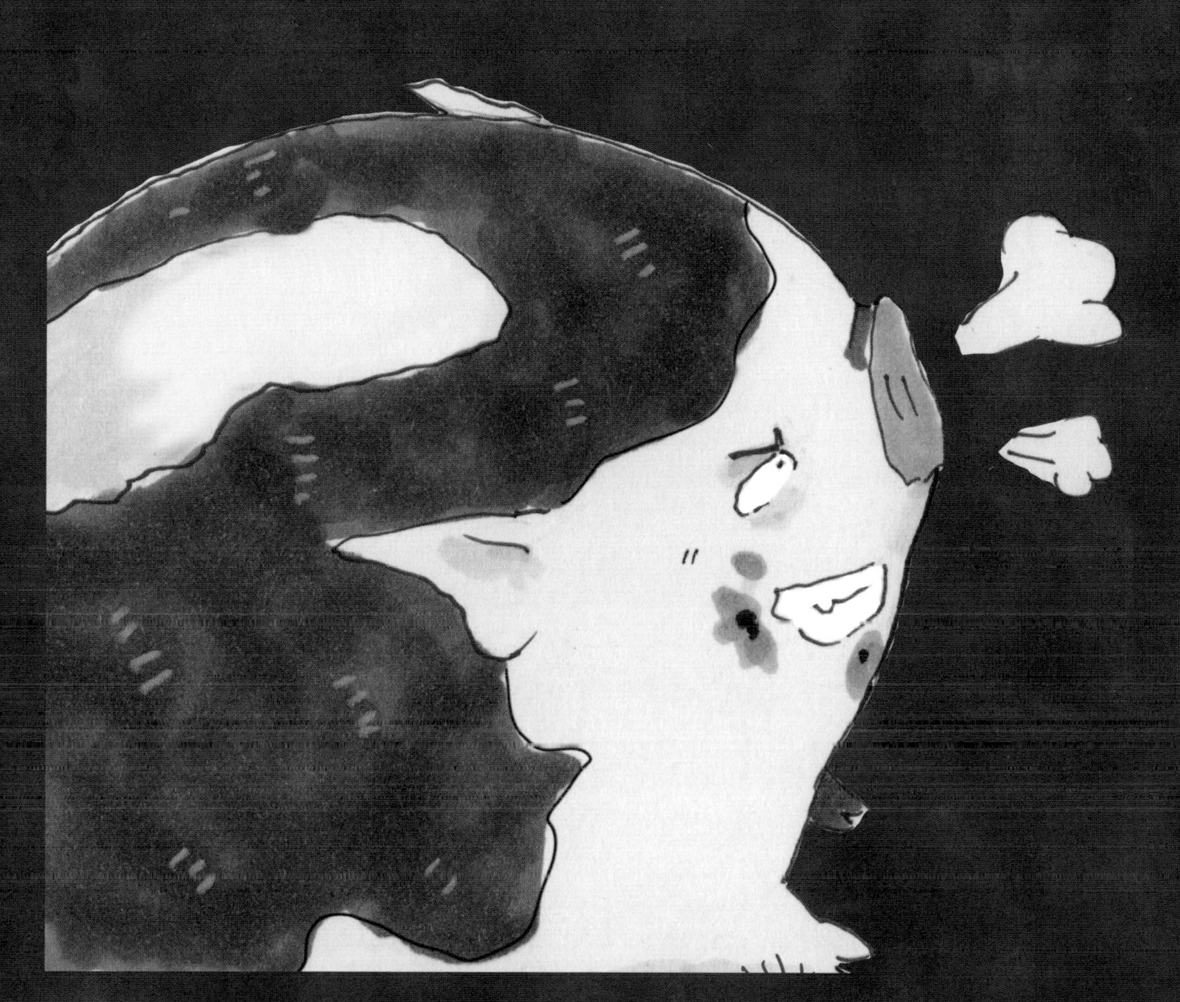

But she continued screaming, "It's a pig! It's a f*cking pig!"

Over and over again. And it was starting to irritate him.

So Wilbur grunted. Loudly.

Then he heard dogs barking within the house. That wasn't so good.

When the woman went back inside, he decided to be on his way.

But he didn't know where he was. Or where he was going.

So he just stood there instead.

Wilbur then went back to licking the grill. Because why not.

It was good. And he wanted to.

But the woman came out the door again. This time with a dog's leash.

He felt the leash slip over his head.

"What the ..." warned Wilbur. "Oh no you don't."

He dug in, squealing.

But the woman was strong. And Wilbur was not as strong.

And somehow he landed behind a fence in a paddock on her property.

At least he wouldn't have to see his kids again. It wasn't so bad he thought.

So that is where he stayed.

He couldn't leave anyway. Because of the damn fence.

One day, the woman believed he needed a friend.

So she brought him a donkey. Which he hated.

The donkey was ugly. And it stunk. It was also dumb.

So Wilbur attacked the donkey with his sharp, tusk-like teeth.

He bit the donkey's butt and legs really hard.

The donkey screamed and bled a lot.

But Wilbur didn't care.

"You're SUCH an asshole," the woman screamed at Wilbur, as she led the bleeding donkey out of the paddock.

"That would be correct," said Wilbur.

And he went back to being alone.

Because he liked it that way.

Months went by.

One day Wilbur awoke in his paddock face down in the dirt, and felt a pang in his heart.

Was it the watermelon she gave him? Or perhaps the pluots?

Maybe the woman was trying to kill him.

But this didn't feel so much like indigestion. Or a poisoning.

It was something different. It was more of an. . .

Emptiness?

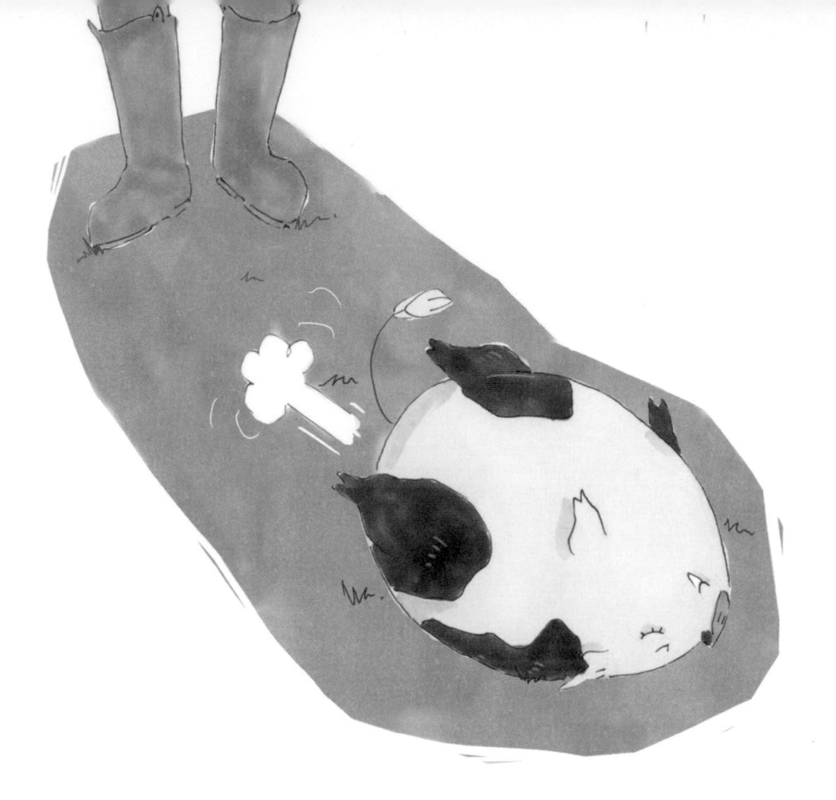

The woman visited him every day. And every day, she looked more concerned.

"What's wrong, Wilbur?" she'd ask sympathetically.

"What's wrong, Wilbur," he'd mimic, rolling on his back and farting.

But something was wrong. And he couldn't put his hoof on it.

The woman didn't know what to do for Wilbur.

What she did know is that she wanted to farm her own eggs, so she needed to raise some baby chickens.

She visited a nearby farm and bought some chicks.

Perhaps they could provide Wilbur with some company.

The chicks lived in Wilbur's paddock in a chicken coop. And he hated them too.

Wilbur watched the chicks grow into young chickens.

"You're dumb, you ugly chickens," he'd yell in the direction of the coop. "Bock, bock, bock."

He was still out of sorts.

And he was being more of an asshole than usual.

If that was possible.

One fall day, as Wilbur was munching on his slop, he noticed that one of the chickens wasn't quite like the others.

For one thing, it was huge. It had a big red blob of something under its neck and another red blob on its head that waggled when it walked.

For another thing, it was always pecking at the coop door.

The incessant pecking was starting to drive Wilbur crazy.

"What are you OCD or something?" thought Wilbur.

"You are truly one ugly chicken," Wilbur shouted at the coop before lolling back on his straw.

"And you've got something on your head," he said, signaling to the red wobbly blob.

"That's because I'm not a chicken you asshole," said the chicken, peck, peck, pecking at the door.

Wilbur couldn't believe his ears. Had that ugly chicken just talked back to him?

He snorted and prepared to give the chicken some donkey medicine.

You talkin' to me?

I'm talkin' to you.

You talkin' to me?!

I'm talkin' to you.

Me?

Yes, YOU.

Wilbur couldn't believe his ears.

Or his eyes. The damned chicken was huge—super puffed up.

Like it was on steroids or something.

It stared at Wilbur right through the coop door and cocked its head to the side.

And then it smiled weirdly, as the coop door flew open into Wilbur's paddock.

Wilbur's eyes widened. Pretty much as widely as they could.

"Oh sh*t."

The ugly chicken flew out of the coop and started chasing Wilbur.

Wilbur squealed and ran around his paddock with the damn chicken in hot pursuit.

"Raphael!" Wilbur heard the woman scream as she came racing out her back door. For the first time, Wilbur was happy to see the woman.

He thought maybe the stupid chicken would chase her instead.

As the woman raced into the paddock, Wilbur ran behind her to get out of the way of the crazy chicken.

Raphael dove into the woman's shins with his sharp beak.

"AAAAAAAGGGGGG!" screamed the woman, batting the rooster away. "You asshole!"

Wilbur was just happy that the big, ugly chicken was no longer chasing him.

The woman looked at the pig and the rooster who were now standing side by side.

"You know something?" she asked.

But her question was rhetorical as she quickly replied, "You're both assholes."

She limped away angrily holding her shin.

Wilbur stood there dazed, looking warily at what was clearly no chicken.

Was she going to leave that thing in his paddock?

Days went by, and Raphael remained in the paddock, as he would not remain in the coop.

Raphael and Wilbur gradually reached a detente.

Wilbur didn't always mind the stupid rooster.

Sometimes they chatted about the weather, and the fact that they both hated pluots and chickens.

So they had that in common.

But Wilbur's heart didn't seem to feel quite as empty either.

The weird feeling he had experienced so many moons ago had mysteriously melted away.

One day, they both watched from the paddock as the woman returned to the farm with a fat, old, female dog that resembled something from another planet.

"Gidget," they could hear the woman coo, "I know it's been a hard life at the pound, but now you will be free. I already have an adoptive home for you!"

She led the dog into the red barn next to the paddock.

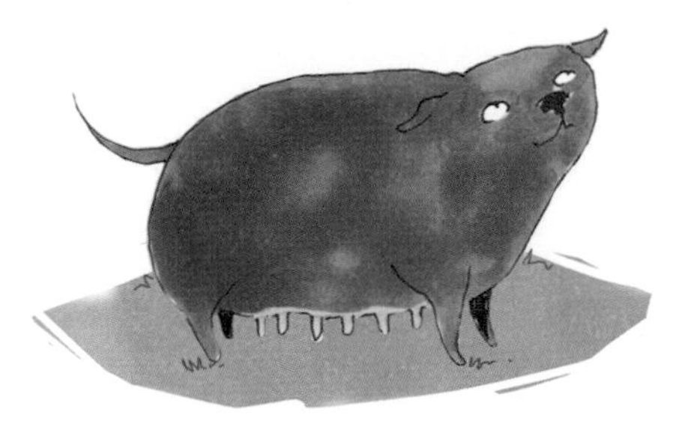

"Good, the dumb dog will be leaving soon," said Raphael. "That one looks like she's had a million kids. I hate dogs."

"Yeah," said Wilbur, "I hate dogs too."

So they had that in common.

The next day, the woman brought Gidget to her new home.

"How sweet!" Gidget's adoptive mother beamed. "What a pretty girl. She'll make a wonderful addition to our family!"

A few days later, Raphael and Wilbur watched with consternation as the woman brought Gidget back to the farm.

Gidget was returning to the red barn because she hated all the dogs in her new home. So she bit them.

Then she decided to bite her new family members.

Because why not.

Gidget pretty much hated everyone.

Well, everyone, except for the woman.

And Gidget had weird habits, like rolling in sh*t.
Didn't matter whose.

So Gidget came back to the farm, the red barn and the
woman she loved.

The woman gave Gidget a bath.

Then took her for a walk
around the farm as Raphael
and Wilbur watched from
the paddock.

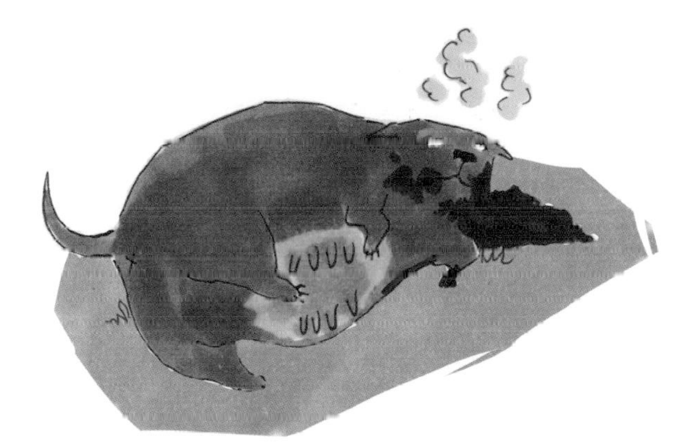

The squeaky clean Gidget
rolled in a large pile
of sh*t.

"Noooo!!!" screamed the woman.
"Why do you do that??!!"

Gidget smiled and pranced
proudly along covered in sh*t.

Because that's the way
she rolled.

Wilbur and Raphael both rolled over laughing at the woman's despair.

They had just finished a long argument about who of the two was the bigger asshole.

And they had at that time agreed that between Raphael and Wilbur, they were equally big assholes!

But they were forced to reopen their debate after witnessing Gidget waddling along covered in sh*t.

And they both agreed: Gidget was the biggest asshole of them all! And the stinkiest!

The woman decided
that Gidget was Gidget.

She would always be full
of sh*t and that was the
way it was.

As for Raphael and Wilbur,
the woman visits them
daily with a protective
stick just in case they
decide to be assholes.

And all the assholes lived happily ever after on the farm in New Jersey.

The End.

Or is it?

THE REAL ASSHOLES OF NEW JERSEY

Wilbur

Raphael

Gidget

THE AUTHORS & ILLUSTRATOR

Founder of Diamonds in the Ruff Dog Rescue, a certified dog trainer and talented mixologist, with a master's in Business Admin, ERICA BROWN has provided and found homes for creatures great and small for many, many years, including all of the assholes in this book. She shares her home on eight acres of farmland in New Jersey with her three rescue dogs, 16 chickens and a pig.

For S.J. RUSSELL her love for animals runs deep; she is especially inspired by the ill-mannered and ill-tempered. A writer and attorney, Russell shares her Philly home with a patient spouse and enough cats to solidify her cat lady status as "crazy."

MAGGIE MCMAHON is a Philadelphia artist who loves animals 'n sh*t. She shares her home with a rescued pure Phillybred dog from the city's open-intake shelter and has two cats straight off the streets of Philly.

Archimedes' Printing Shoppe
& Sundry Goodes

Disclaimer: This is a work of mostly nonfiction. In fact, the names, characters and incidences have not been changed one bit: They all refer to the actual assholes in this book. Notwithstanding, any resemblance to any other pigs, roosters, chickens, dogs, eggs (unborn chickens) or assholes, living or dead, or actual places, events, incidents or businesses is purely coincidental.

the pen
the house